I0065122

SpotZ The Frenchie

SpotZ The Frenchie

SpotZ The Frenchie

SpotZ The Frenchie

SpotZ The Frenchie

SpotZ The Frenchie

SpotZ The Frenchie

SpotZ The Frenchie

SpotZ The Frenchie

SpotZ The Frenchie

SpotZ The Frenchie

SpotZ The Frenchie

SpotZ The Frenchie

SpotZ The Frenchie

SpotZ The Frenchie

SpotZ The Frenchie

SpotZ The Frenchie

SpotZ The Frenchie

SpotZ The Frenchie

SpotZ The Frenchie

SpotZ The Frenchie

SpotZ The Frenchie

SpotZ The Frenchie

SpotZ The Frenchie

SpotZ The Frenchie

SpotZ The Frenchie

SpotZ The Frenchie

SpotZ The Frenchie

SpotZ The Frenchie

SpotZ The Frenchie

SpotZ The Frenchie

SpotZ The Frenchie

SpotZ The Frenchie

SpotZ The Frenchie

SpotZ The Frenchie

SpotZ The Frenchie

SpotZ The Frenchie

SpotZ The Frenchie

SpotZ The Frenchie

SpotZ The Frenchie

SpotZ The Frenchie

SpotZ The Frenchie

SpotZ The Frenchie

SpotZ The Frenchie

SpotZ The Frenchie

SpotZ The Frenchie

SpotZ The Frenchie

SpotZ The Frenchie

SpotZ The Frenchie

SpotZ The Frenchie

Spot Z The Frenchie

SpotZ The Frenchie

SpotZ The Frenchie

SpotZ The Frenchie

www.ingramcontent.com/pod-product-compliance
Lightning Source LLC
Chambersburg PA
CBHW081822200326

41597CB00023B/4347